Teaching Tales

Lessons and Laughter from a Christian School

Jami and Niki Roethe

PublishAmerica
Baltimore

First printing

ISBN: 1-60610-137-4
PUBLISHED BY PUBLISHAMERICA, LLLP
www.publishamerica.com
Baltimore

Printed in the United States of America

Teaching Tales

Lessons and Laughter
from a Christian School

Literary Disclaimer

This book is a collection of memories from nine years of teaching in a tiny Christian school in Southern Illinois. The names of the children have been changed to protect the innocent, or in some cases, guilty, but the thoughts and actions are purely their own.

Although children have been quoted in this volume, the quotes are merely our recollections of past events and are not particular to any one child.

Acknowledgments

We dedicate these writings to all of those in the field of education who strive each day to make the future just a little bit brighter for the lives of America's children. Only ones who have served in the trenches with you, know how hard you work. Keep up the good fight as you strive to educate the future leaders of this country. May you always feel appreciated.

This collection is also dedicated to Jim and Susan Roethe and the rest of our family and friends who have stood by us during this time of triumphs and trials. May we always make you proud. We are truly grateful for your never-ending love and support. May God always bless and keep you close.

To Pat and Mike for your fabulous photography and unfailing support.

Thanks also to the folks of Lancaster Christian School. We are ever grateful for the opportunities and the memories. God Bless!

What Is a Teacher?

The other day I saw a sweatshirt in one of the many catalogs I receive every day that said, "The best parts about teaching are June, July, and August." I'm not sure why that disturbed me, but it did. I'm sure that the catalog company thought that their saying was very cute and they will sell lots of sweatshirts because of it. However, I am a teacher and I find the idea that the only reason I teach is for a few months off offensive. When I was in college during my "teacher prep" courses, I encountered another student who was chronically late for class, complained often about the kids she was "stuck with" during school placements and never had assignments completed on time. Finally, I asked her why she was becoming a teacher when she obviously could not stand teaching.

She replied, "Summers and all major holidays off!"

I lost touch with that student when the class was over and I never heard whether she got a teaching job or not, but I sincerely hope not.

Unfortunately, society often views teachers like this former college student. I have even heard some state that all teachers have to do is sit there and watch a few kids every day and then collect a paycheck. People see teachers as "whiners" when they ask for more pay or benefits or if they ask to be treated like the professionals they are. Citizens often resent the money spent on schools and don't mind telling instructors that they are merely wasting tax dollars. Maybe that is true for a few instructors; however, I can say from personal experience, that most teachers are highly educated and motivated individuals who are just trying to make a difference. There is not another profession, unless perhaps it would be the Presidency, which has such a direct influence on such a wide variety of our population as teaching. Teachers can honestly say that they get to touch the future every single day.

To those who would still condemn teachers, I'd just like to say this, "Have you visited a school lately? Do you know what teachers do?"

Dedicated teachers often get to work early and stay late without the promise of overtime pay. They try to teach morals and values such as respect and responsibility when many of their students are not taught this at home. Teachers have a huge range of abilities in their classroom. All students are expected to achieve and have individual attention, which is hard, when due to cost cutting, there are more children than ever in each classroom. Teachers are expected to administer state tests, many written by "experts" who have never taught and or haven't set foot in a classroom for years. If the students do not do well, instructors are held accountable. Teachers have become experts at jumping through hoops to satisfy parents, and even state officials who feel that the problems with the country today can be traced right back to the schools. They get to be traffic cops, mothers, fathers, nurses, counselors, pastors, secretaries, and even janitors— all in the name of educating America's youth. They spend their own money for classroom supplies and further education. Teachers are extremely active in extra curricular school activities and community events, doing most without extra pay. Most go home to kids of their own after dealing with other children all day. And teachers do this, on one of the lowest salary rates of any job in the country. For these dedicated individuals, the greatest "perks" of teaching do not include "summers off."

During summers, like most teachers I try to catch up on the many activities that got pushed aside during the teaching year. I see parents with their kids at the stores, and I wonder if they appreciate teachers after getting a little taste of what instructors see every day. In a few short weeks schools will once again be filled with the laughter of children and the voices of their teachers. The future leaders will be filling those desks and a large part of who they will become will depend on the individuals standing by the chalkboards. Instructors will once again take up the task of shaping the country, and they will do it, to the very best of their abilities.

If you appreciate a teacher be sure to say so.

Why I Teach

I could not do my job if I were all alone.
They have so many problems that soon become my own.
There are so many worries, and so many cares.
I would be overwhelmed, if I thought that You weren't there.
This one has a troubled home. That one cannot add.
She still can't tie her shoes. I have a meeting with his dad.
I go from day today imparting knowledge to the young.
And I know that in my heart, the battle has just begun.
I don't just work with the children, but their families as well.
That's a big responsibility, and without You, I would fail.
The hours are long. The pay is meager.
And sometimes the students are far from eager.
I have to remember the kids belong to You.
Help me to focus on that in everything I do.
My goal is that someday toward Your love they'll reach.
That's the ultimate gift that I can give. And that is why I teach.

The School

The classrooms are quiet—Yet unbroken by the sounds of young voices clamoring for all sorts of attentions. The building waits as if it already anticipates the coming pounding of feet down its hallways and the slamming metal clang of locker doors as teachers' voices rise above the din with the daily caution, "Don't run! Don't run!"

Here the school sits waiting even as the hands of various clocks inch closer to the inevitable 8:15 deadline where the small voices that have steadily been growing in variety and volume as they are held in the aging gymnasium wait for the call, "The bus is here." Then, these small "early birds" will join their later counterparts in the buzzing swarm that will migrate down the hallway as packs breaks off to visit the restroom or the water fountain. As if ready for the coming horde, the compressor on the water fountain creaks to life with the promise of providing cool beverage for small, parched throats.

8:10-Anticipation builds as the slamming wooden door becomes increasingly frequent as more show up for another day. Teachers wait in the hall with what they hope are bright, if not slightly weary smiles to welcome their charges. 8:15 arrives, no turning back now as the building embraces the loud chorus of voices, swinging backpacks, dragging coats and morning greetings as children head into classrooms for another day. Slowly the hallway din diminishes as the children sort themselves into their respective spots. Classroom doors squeak closed as the final stragglers make their way to their rooms.

The hallways are quieter now. The chorus of voices is subdued behind doors as instructors train their charges. The building holds them gently as it watches and waits for the time of release.

It is not an overly impressive building. Bricks have cracked slightly. Paint has peeled a little. The tiled floors have lost much of their shine. No, the building would not generally receive a second glance but for one thing. It is just four walls, but it holds the future inside.

Tales in the Lunch Room

In many schools, instructors usher their charges into a cafeteria type environment and then can cheerfully wander back to their classrooms or into the teachers' lounge for a meal of their own. Some even are allowed to leave the school's campus for a little down time for themselves. Other schools, like ours, require teachers to not only eat their meals in the same room as the children, but elbow to elbow with their young charges. Of course, eating with the students has taught some invaluable lessons. For example, I have learned to never wear white on spaghetti, or chili days, and to choose spots carefully on days when ketchup bottles are present since some children squeeze the red sauce with much zeal and no common sense. Sometimes, during more stressful moments, I have to admit I resent the fact that some teachers seem to have so much more free time than I have, and yet, I realize that my life is much richer because of conversations like the following.

* * * * * * * * * *

While sitting between a kindergarten student and his second grade sister, the much older and wiser sibling informed me that her brother let Cinnamon, the family dog, lick his face. I was thinking of the appropriate response to this bit of information.

The kindergarten student chose this moment and chimed in, "Yeah, and Cinny licks her butt too!"

I almost choked on my spaghetti. His voice was so matter of fact. I had trouble even forming an appropriate verbal response.

My aide, however, after recovering from her bout of suppressed shock (and laughter), said severely, "That is precisely why you shouldn't let your doggie lick your face."

* * * * * * * * * *

In another "close conversation of the weird kind," two of the second and third grade students were discussing a cousin of one who went to a different school.

Apparently, the supply of brain waves was kind of short that day because one student looked at the other and said, "Huh, West Salem Public School. Is that the school you go to?"

To this, the student to whom she was speaking and fellow member of HER OWN CLASS, just looked at her like she had come from Mars, which as the conversation went on, we were sure she had!

My sister, quick to correct the erring student said, "He doesn't go to that school. He is in your class!"

To that the brain challenged child replied, "How do you know? Is the other school the one you teach at?"

My sister continued. "I am YOUR teacher. Your friend is in YOUR Class!! Where are we right now?"

You could almost count the clicks as the slow burning light bulb in the child's brain lit up.

"Duh," she said laughing loudly, "What was I thinking?"

What indeed!

* * * * * * * * * *

It is also amazing what students will consider a "lunch". Recently during a celebration of the 100th day of school, one student was especially creative. Fruit Roll Ups were a part of the celebration earlier that morning, or, as we like to put it: sticky, thin fruit flavored pieces of simulated plastic. Anyway when we arrived at the lunch table for another culinary delight, one of the sixth graders informed his stressed out teacher that he had forgotten that he had brought his lunch. His unsuspecting instructor viewed the held lunch box and sighed as its presence would mean changing the lunch count and confessing the oversight to the chief cook. The instructor dealt with the "extra dished up plate" fiasco and finally got to sit down. She then discovered that the child's "meal" consisted of a Fruit Roll Up and 100 marshmallows left over from the morning's math lesson. Needless to say, that did NOT go over very well.

* * * * * * * * * *

Dealing with picky eaters is always a challenge. What happens when the school's dietary chef discovers that she forgot to purchase the lettuce to go with the spaghetti? She decides to serve peas with the Italian entrée. One *extremely* picky eater decided that he was only going to eat the bread that went with the meal. This was fine until he discovered that the offensive sauce from the heavily cooked pasta had contaminated the one favorable thing on his plate. As he held the offensive bread high in the air he expressed much concern because his finger and his garlic bread had touched the red stuff.

His stressed educator said, "Just eat it! You won't die because the bread has a drop of sauce on it."

He did! He breathes still!

* * * * * * * * * *

Did you know that potato chips were dangerous? I'm not talking about cholesterol or anything like that.

Apparently anyone who consumes chips is at risk of getting the dreaded “tongue cuts”.

I wasn’t aware of this affliction until one of my students, while consuming a chip, remarked, “I’m not really used to eating chips, ’cause of the cuts they put on my tongue with the sharp edges. They taste pretty good, though.”

If you needed something new to worry about, now you can worry about tongue cuts! Potato chips can be lethal!

* * * * * * * * * * *

Sometimes, it is not necessarily the food in the lunchroom that causes the conversation. It is merely the location for conversations like this.

Student One—“My body feels really different right now.”

Student Two—“Different in a good way, or a bad way?”

Student One—“I don’t know, but I think I need some water.”

Student Two—“Well, ask Miss Roethe if you can go get some and leave me alone.”

Student One, after leaving to get a drink of water and coming back, “My body doesn’t feel different any more. I’m a-okay now!”

Student Two—“I’m glad for you, really I am.”

(Now, we did not even ask what made the Student One’s body feel “different.” Sometimes ignorance really is bliss.)

* * * * * * * * * * *

One day in the lunch room, we had spaghetti and meat sauce which the children enjoy immensely, though we teachers learned really quickly not to wear light colored clothing during the “slurp fest.” Because the noodles were often done very early, the cook usually left them soaking in the boiling water so that the pasta wouldn't stick together and rival the size of drinking straws by the time we got around to eating lunch. When placed on the plate, the noodles seemed to "float" in their own juices and the sauce had no desire to stick to them. Apparently, this wasn't that big of problem for the children who always managed to slurp down large quantities of this culinary delight.

One of the kindergarteners did have an interesting comment, however, "Teacher, can I go get some more noodles? This time I want some clean, dry ones."

While the cook was not amused by this request, the child did get his clean noodles. As for them, they were a whole lot less "slimy" when dried on a paper napkin.

* * * * * * * * * *

Like most schools across the country, our students dine on foods from the government lunch program. While this is not altogether a bad thing, sometimes the quality of the foodstuffs could be better. Most of the time the children do not seem to mind, but at other times, their blunt honesty just shines through.

When one youngster eyed the purple cabbage that had infested his lettuce salad, he commented to the cook, "Do ya' think you could please take that purpley stuff off my salad. It tastes nasty and makes me gassy."

She was a little offended, but he did say "please."

In another instance, the students were eying the semi-clear yellowish chicken gravy that was being ladled over the snowy white globs of instant mashed potatoes. (Now, our students are big fans of the brown beef gravy, but I can't blame them when they think the chicken gravy is less than appealing. Of course, thanks to one careful comment, now it's really not a nice thought.)

The student fumbled for the right words as the cook dished up his plate, but as she reached over to spoon the gravy over his spuds, he blurted out, “Please, can’t I eat them plain without the snot?”

Field Trip Fun

It was a simple field trip idea. Tour a local planetarium and train museum. Of course when you work in a school in the middle of nowhere, "local" means anything less than three hours away. The students enjoyed the planetarium, except they weren't very wild about it being dark. They also did not like it when the lady running the show caused the stars to move around the ceiling. This caused the feeling of spinning.

As one of the students stated, "Save me Lord! My seats a movin'."

The children also enjoyed seeing all of the trains. They got to walk through a dining car and sit in a caboose. Of course not all of our students were in the same tour group. By luck, good or bad, the younger set got a Grandpa Jones type character who had plenty of time to answer every question and let them touch everything, even the things that said, "Do not touch." The older group ended up with the Wicked Witch of the West. These students were not allowed to ask questions or explore any area of the museum that was not on this lady's flight plan.

As one of the sixth graders put it afterward, "What was with that lady? She was like 'I hate my job. I hate my life. I may even hate you guys a little.'"

Unfortunately, he was fairly accurate. Fortunately, he did not express his opinion to the tour guide's face, but at the same time, it would have been nice if he had not been so nice in public! The day was saved, however, when the bus took the children to a huge playground and turned them loose. After quickly gulping down sack lunches the kids played with cheerful abandon, leaving their teachers to pick up and pack up all of the coolers. Some of the students even fell asleep on the way home. That is proof positive that there is a God!

* * * * * * * * * *

Taking students on a field trip is always an adventure. Once we took our students to a fairly close historic park and let them tour authentic log cabins. They really enjoyed seeing all of the craftspeople make candles, weave cloth and baskets, assemble shoes and wash clothes with a washboard while using homemade soap. All of the children were amazed that people actually used to, not only survive, but also flourish without cell phones, TV, video games and trampolines, not to mention indoor plumbing!

Just when we thought they had gotten the concept, one came up with this poignant statement, “Yeah making clothes is cool and all, but if you got tired of that, you just went to Wal-mart, right?”

* * * * * * * * * *

When working on an extremely tight budget, one is always on the lookout for fun and inexpensive field trip ideas. We thought that we came up with the perfect solution. Let’s take kids to the local national park. The admission is free and all of the students will fit in either the church van or our personal vehicle. It sounded just great! All the kids would need to bring would be two dollars for ice cream at a local ice cream parlor and a sack lunch.

The plans were made. A park ranger even planned to take us on our own personal tour through the woods and answer any questions the students might have. Hallelujah! At last someone who could satisfy the kid's insatiable thirst for woodland knowledge!

All the permission slips were sent out and returned. Lunches were packed. Drivers for vehicles were secured. The big day arrived! One slight setback. Instead of the "beautiful fall day" that we planned, the weather was a sunny 40 degrees with a blustery northern wind! No matter. We could dress the kids warmer. Even the fact that a large storm had taken out power in the visitor's center the night before couldn't dampen the adventurous spirit!

We loaded the explorers into their respective vehicles and we were off! All, especially for the three students in my car that sang at the top of their lungs the whole time, made the ride in relative comfort. Upon our arrival the students enjoyed playing on the playground in spite of the brisk wind chill. We then trooped through the woods with our guide who just wanted the kids to "shut up" by the time we emerged an hour and a half later.

On to lunch— After all the fresh air, the students were *really* hungry. Unfortunately, we chose our picnic spot unwisely because most of the students had portions of their lunch consumed by some over zealous geese! Just to add to the excitement, one child's lunch box blew into the lake and his brother gamely jumped in to save it! While he was placed in front of the car heater to dry out, another student guzzled a "big gulp" soda. Too much "goose fear" and "getting left" anxiety led to the "big gulp" being sprayed all over the picnic area prior to departure. Apparently though, the afflicted student suffered no ill effects because he ordered himself a large ice cream when we stopped for it instead of the 7-UP that I would have preferred.

Some memories just can't be washed away no matter how hard you try! One that will never disappear is what occurred upon our arrival back at the school. Due to all of the "unexpected events" we arrived back earlier than expected. We had all of the kids in one warm classroom and put in a *Disney* tape. *Each one fell asleep!* It is times like these when you learn to thank God for small favors!

* * * * * * * * * * *

Once we took our kiddos to awesome Albion, IL to experience the sights of Citizen's National Bank and the Edward's County courthouse. We ended up having to take two vehicles due to a bus mix up, putting all of the K-1 class on one mini bus and the 2-5 group on the church van. The event was looked upon with much anticipation as the kids toted in their sack lunches. My students were fairly well controlled until we passed a pasture complete with a few mules. There, the owners of the pasture had placed three large crosses on the side of their hill.

My children's excitement knew no bounds as one explained. "Wow! I didn't think the cross where Jesus died would still look so good. We should get out and get flowers or somethin'."

The whole group responded to this enthusiastically. I was a little confused and asked the students if they honestly thought that we had actually passed the true cross of Christ and that we had gone all the way to Jerusalem.

One of my more outspoken students stated, "We HAVE been traveling a long time!"

(Note: We had traveled for a whopping total of 35 minutes.) After our trip to "Jerusalem" the bank and courthouse were almost dull.

* * * * * * * * * * *

Once we took the students to another local school to attend a "wild bird show." The children were very excited to see the hawks and owls that flew around the gym to alight onto the protected gloved hands of their handlers for the little bits of bird treats. The kids were awed by the birds in flight except for the third grade student who sat next to one of her teachers. She exhibited true terror, all be it quiet terror as the only real evidence of her fear was the claw marks in her instructor's arm for a week.

And then came Izzy. Perhaps the most ugly bird ever created, Izzy was an African vulture complete with a red bald head and bright blue eyes. He was new to the program which may be the main cause of the calamity when Izzy went crazy and started whipping around the gym like a paper airplane on drugs, slamming into the bleachers and totally ignoring the outstretched hands of the handlers. Apparently, flying around at break neck speeds was more exciting than the little meat niblets in the gloved hands of the two women trying to catch him.

On one of his last passes before capture, he swooped incredibly low and managed to touch his horny little talons to the top of one teacher's head. It was not a good time for the instructor. (By the way, she lives still and is one of the ones responsible for the tales you are reading.) And all of this was in the name of education!

It's a New Day

The day is starting again Lord. Am I in the right frame of mind?

Christmas break has been over for two days. Get ready to hear the whine.

The lunch offering today is something they are sure to hate,

And the weather means no one can go out to play.

It's our day to clean the school again, and there is sure to be a fuss,

Because everyone likes to vacuum and no one likes to dust.

Everyone is tired, trying to fit back into the routine.

Sometimes tempers flare and voices are quite mean.

Please grant me patience, Lord. Help me to find their joy.

Help me to do my best for every girl and boy.

I have been entrusted with these children for just a little while.

Help me be willing to go the extra mile.

Lord, help me find the blessing that each child is to me.

Thank you, Lord for another gift; the clock just now says "3:00!"

A Clean School Is a Happy School

Part of teaching involves teaching students values such as responsibility and teamwork. Sometimes instead of just talking about attributes a teacher would like to see in his or her students, a more "hands on" approach is needed. That is why our private school instigated the Elementary Student Cleaning Policy. One a month, students clean the entire school and each day a student takes a turn "bussing" the tables in the lunchroom. These are great ideas, but not with out a few little "twists."

* * * * * * * * * * *

After assigning each of the Kindergarten and First grade students a job cleaning the students eagerly began their appointed tasks. I was busy supervising the zealot who was cleaning off my desk, and missed the kindergarten student on "dust patrol." She worked very hard to empty an entire can of lemon furniture polish on her rag to dust with. The overpowering smell of lemon alerted me to the problem too late. The rag practically dripped with spray and the young miss was standing in an area of my tiled floor that now looked like highly polished glass.

Although we scrubbed the floor thoroughly, that area of the floor had a finish for days that would make an icicle proud!

During the Open House that occurred that night, I spent all of my time saying, "Oh, be careful! Don't walk here! Watch your step!"

I must say though, that my dusting child was extremely proud of herself.

"Look, Mommy!" she said. "I made our floor like a mirror!"

Mirror indeed!

* * * * * * * * * *

One of the most coveted jobs on the cleaning grew each month is the "dust moppers." If you want to see real power, pass out two large sized rag mops and let the kids start pushing. Two of our cleaners got a little more than they bargained for when they actually got to do someone else's job over again. The boys decided to reenact a fierce battle from the movie "Star Wars" by brandishing the mops over their shoulders and jousting each other with their "light sabers." While the battle was decidedly fearsome complete with billowing clouds of floor dust every time the two mop heads connected, the boys did not count on what would happen when they got caught.

Because of the generous spreading of dust from their battle, the boys ended up getting to re-dust the church pews in the entry of the school as well as re-vacuum the entry rugs. Needless to say, those two boys missed most of their recess as they cleaned up the aftermath of their galactic war!

* * * * * * * * * *

The trash detail is another envious occupation as the team gets to push around a sixty-gallon trash receptacle on wheels. On one occasion, the two students on this team were decidedly inept at their job. The students were very zealous in pushing the big trashcan, but they lacked the skills, or the smarts, to successfully pull it off.

First, we had to show them how to tilt the container back so that the wheels would give the optimum benefit. Before we showed them this, the two were shoving the can flat on the floor causing a horrendous scuffing noise. Of course, this led to the tip that even when you tilt the can back, you must still hold to the handle, or gravity will cause it to go "boom" spilling the contents. (This was learned through the trial and error method as trash was spilled several times before the students finally learned to grasp the handle firmly as they tilted the garbage can backwards.)

The boys also were not that great at steering the trashcan even though both were tall enough to see over the top of their trash vehicle. As they barreled toward the school's library, they banged right into my sister as she stood in the doorway directing the chalkboard cleaners and dusters. Undeterred, instead of looking to see that she was blocking the path and deciding to wait patiently, they backed up across the hallway to take a running start, blasting into her at full throttle.

It was not their finest moment as on impact, they released the handle of the tilted can letting it slam into the floor spilling trash liberally across the hallway.

Although Jami was not injured in the collision, the boys' pride was not as fortunate as they were removed from the trash team for the year!

* * * * * * * * * *

One Teacher Institute day, the three L.C.S. teachers cleaned out the two old locker rooms used for storage. I know that some of the stuff in those rooms had not been touched in twenty years except for the "feetsies" of the gray small-legged critters that like to visit occasionally. Luckily, in all of our rummaging, we didn't see any of the gray visitors either alive, or dead. Whew! God is Good!

Anyhow, in all of the cleaning out, we managed to make quite a name for L.C.S. with the local garbage collectors with all of the (pardon the language) C-R-A-P we hauled out. In the first load, I carried out twenty plastic molded kid sized lawn chairs someone donated. While I am sure the donations made someone feel really good about himself or herself, we had climbed around them for at least seven years and I was finished. Still, I could not just throw them out, so I stacked them by the dumpster with a sign that said, "Free." Sure enough, within a half an hour, all of the chairs were gone as well as the Little Tykes kitchen set that had been busted in the back!

We also dug out many paper Burger King crowns that had been used in some long past Christmas play. Of course, all it took was one child wearing a crown out on the playground and the kindergarten class was on those paper treasures like fleas on a hound dog. Before you could say, "Hail to the Chief," those kids had crowns fitted to their own little skulls and were gamely trying to cram them onto their unsuspecting classmates. One girl even managed to get hers on her head by sticking her two pigtails out the top! Talk about the ultimate fashion statement! She looked as if the aliens had definitely landed.

The crown treasures led into much "dumpster diving' that the teachers had to quickly put a stop to. Could you imagine the parents' faces if their beloved youngster would have come home dragging a huge box of mouse nibbled felt squares or twenty year old plaster molds? It almost would have been worth it!

* * * * * * * * * *

During Earth Day celebrations, we usually have the elementary students don latex gloves and walk a few blocks picking up trash along the roadways around the school. This always has led to a lot of fun such as the time when a kindergarten student hauled a whole truck mat out of the watery ditch, carefully dried it on the grass, and then tried to use it as a sled to shimmy down the hill next to a local cemetery.

Of course, one of the crowning memories of those times was the first grade student that spent more time waving at passing cars than actually gathering trash.

When a lady in a large Cadillac refused to acknowledge his latex clad hand waving, he screamed as she passed, "That was really rude, Lady. Rude people go to Hell!"

I don't think she heard him, but she sure knew where he was from as he was wearing his blazing yellow L.C.S. t-shirt!

Welcome to Class! You Can Start Thinking Now!

Kids never cease to amaze me at their utter lack of brain cell function at times. It seems as if they are struck by moments of brilliance in the midst of seas of stupidity. These next stories, while certainly humorous, are not the brilliant variety.

One student was in charge of filling a cup with water from the drinking fountain. She gamely took the container and got ready to forge out of the room to fulfill her task. Unfortunately, when she got to the door instead of opening it out into the hallway, she yanked the doorknob back toward her with much force. As it did not open as she expected, she braced her large flip flop clad feet against the door and again pulled inward hard. Now, it doesn't take a rocket scientist to realize she is trying to open the door the wrong way. Of course no one ever accused this child of being a rocket scientist anyway. So here she is yanking and swinging from the doorknob as the rest of the class watches in perplexed amazement.

"Teacher! Someones a holdin' on the door and pullin' it to keep me in."

At this point, "teacher", who managed not to laugh out loud went to the door and gently restrained the struggling student before she wrenched the doorknob off completely. She then opened the door out into the hall.

"Oh, I didn't know," the struggling student said.

That was painfully obvious!

* * * * * * * * * * *

Sometimes the best laid out plans manage to go awry. The teacher, that's me, failed to provide one of my groups with information about a city. Knowing that Jami's class had had a book about the fair state of Illinois with some dandy pictures of Chicago in it, I forged across the hall to retrieve the volume. Because Jami was busy, she had her "helper of the day" come to help me find the book.

Said child, asked me what I needed the book for and I explained that my children were working on a project about cities.

As the student grasped the sought for book, she said, "Oh then this book about Illinois will be good. It's got some good pictures of New York City in it somewheres."

Not believing what this fourth grade student had said, I stated something to the effect of, "Now think about that. Why would there be pictures of New York in a book about *Illinois*?"

I thought surely she would redeem herself and correct her mistake. I was wrong.

Grasping the book firmly, she started scanning the pages saying, "Now I know I saw a picture of the Statue of Liberty on one of these pictures." Seeing a picture of Abraham Lincoln, she said, "That doesn't look like the Statue of Liberty, but it's close."

I suppose, because it was a picture of a statue, Mr. Lincoln bore a startling resemblance to Lady Liberty herself.

The rest of the class sat in stunned disbelief until I managed to wrestle the book from her hands without screaming, "Where is your brain?"

I even managed to thank her politely for her help and leave without beating my head on the doorframe on my way out.

Apparently as the "space cadet" serenely left the room to head to the bathroom, one of the more concerned students in Jami's class asked, "Miss Roethe, ain't you gonna' fix her?"

Fix her indeed!

* * * * * * * * * *

One day, one of the students rolled into the classroom at 7:30 a.m. like normal.

While coming through the door, she stopped in her tracks and inquired, "Hey, is that there the Chinese flag?"

At that point, my head swiveled around trying to grasp anything that she could have mistaken for the flag of China.

She added, "No, that white one." perhaps in an effort to help me satisfy her curiosity.

It turned out that the Christian flag was mounted directly behind my bewildered head. By then, I had recovered my powers of speech and somehow I managed to keep my voice calm.

"No, dear, that is the Christian flag. You live in the United States. Why would we have the Chinese flag hanging on our wall?"

"I don't know," replied the child, "I was just wonderin'."

Of course, even as I applauded my calm approach, privately I reflected that this would be a very LONG day for this child. It was definitely not the time to point out that we said the pledge to the Christian flag every day. I just made myself promise that someday, that child would know what the Chinese flag looked like! I also would be certain to stress the word *Christian* every time we said the pledge.

* * * * * * * * * *

The school has received tadpoles for several years, and on rare occasions, the critters actually manage to "frog" before school is out. Because we knew they were coming early one year, we were able to get the aquarium tank ready to receive the aquatic critters before they actually arrived. This meant that the tank was filled with water with the filter running a whole day before the tadpoles actually made their appearance.

It didn't seem to matter much to the children. The mass of bright and shining faces hopped off the bus, rushed in the door and began "oohing and aahing" over the "tadpoles" they could see around the rocks. (The tank was still empty of life.)

They even managed to suck in the school's preacher who was caught staring at the lifeless tank trying to see what had the kids so stirred up. You have to admire the imagination of children.

(By the way, the actual tadpoles caused a little less excitement than the "firstcomers.")

* * * * * * * * * *

During a map activity in the 2nd-5th grade class, one of the fifth graders truly proved how bright he really was.

As he worked with his partner on labeling a map of the United States, he muttered to himself, "Texas is almost the biggest state except for Alaska. And which one is the United one?"

He then looked up to his teacher to inquire, "Which one of these states on the map is named 'United'?"

After "teacher" managed to scrape her jaw off of the floor where it had dropped, she was able to answer him patiently. How would you have answered that one without doing or saying something to have the school review your employment?

Cooking Capers

As a teacher, it is always a good thing if one can relate the concept being studied to some sort of hands on activity.

Toward that end, during a study of the country of Italy, we decided to make mini pizzas out of English muffins.

All was going pretty well even though one of my sister's students was sure he would hate the taste "cause the sauce was gonna be nasty" and one of my kids had already dropped his "sauced" muffin face down on the floor.

The children also thought that the English muffins smelled like baloney. (I'm not sure where that came from.) Anyway, we were putting the muffins on the baking pans to put them into the oven and noticed that one of the students had already consumed half of hers raw! Just in case you're wondering, she thought it was "gross" after it had been heated up! The joys of cooking with children just never end!

* * * * * * * * * *

Once, we celebrated "Turkey Day" by making turkeys out of cookies that we glued together with chocolate icing. Nothing peps up students like a little dose of sugar in the morning.

We also made turkey centerpieces out of potatoes and gumdrops for decoration. Martha Stewart had nothing on us. However, let me point out that you have not seen nasty until you meet one of the sliced potato turkeys after it has ridden around in a Ziploc for a week in a child's backpack. It doesn't exactly scream, "Welcome me into your home and put me on your table!" Gobble, gobble, what fun!

* * * * * * * * * * *

The week before Christmas is always busy, but Jami and I in our infinite wisdom, decided to make it more so. As if surviving a program and a party day were not enough, we decided to cook with our angels not once, but twice.

At first we thought that making popcorn balls would have been most fun. Thankfully, the Big Guy upstairs whispered really loudly, "Are you crazy?" and we quickly changed our minds with the kids making snack mix instead. Still I had enough popcorn and pretzels tossed on my floor to feed at least twelve hulking guys at a Super Bowl party! No matter, when I pointed out that fact to the children, they promptly picked up the scraps off the floor and added them to their Ziploc bagged stashes.

Experts say that people will eat over a pound of dirt in their lifetimes. I suppose that our children wanted to fill their quota sooner!

* * * * * * * * * * *

Moving on to the making of Cherry Delight, which as it turns out was "a delight" for no one in charge. We quickly decided to assign a division of labor with the K-1 class combined with the 4th and 5th grade making the filling while the 2nd and 3rd grade made the crust. It *was* a foolproof plan. And then, came the children!

Jami divided graham crackers into bags for her children to pound into crumbs. The whole school could hear the gusto with which they pulverized their crackers.

The poor honey grahams never stood a chance! Only a few bags busted all over the floor making walking on the tile floor more than a little treacherous. The kids never noticed, as they were too busy tossing melted butter and sugar in with their precious crumbs.

Now move next door to the filling room. My group eagerly mixed the cool whip, powdered sugar, and vanilla. Then came the cream cheese and the electric mixer. The handheld machine fascinated the kids even though it was too powerful for some of the K-1 class to use. However, the fun didn't start until one of my girls was supposed to hand over the mixer to the next one in line. Even though she had been cautioned to leave the mixer in the bowl, she decided to pick it up and point it while it was, of course, running. I was liberally splattered with white goop as the kids shouted for her to stop.

In a moment of panic, perhaps confused by the noise, she ended up targeting my chalkboard as well as the ceiling before I could wrestle it out of her Herculean grip. Who knew that a cheap mixer could fling filling that far? I still get to remember that fine day as sticky is still hanging on my ceiling.

By the time we got the filling on the crust and topped it with cherries, the teachers were whipped and the kids were stoked! Oh, I forgot to mention that in their zeal to help out and see what was going on, the children accidentally knocked an open can of cherry filling onto Jami's floor.

Through it all, the teachers remained mainly calm, cool and collected until sampling time when the kids all enthusiastically begged to "do it again." To that I almost replied, "Sure, we'll do it again when the devil's home gets nice and ice covered." Of course, I didn't want to use quite those words. Luckily, God stuffed His fist in my mouth in the nick of time!

* * * * * * * * * * *

In a recent agriculture lesson, the students made grilled cheese sandwiches as they discussed the different farming products used in the aforementioned sandwich. One of the second graders who has the unique distinction of being among the top three pickiest eaters in the world, made a terrible face as he was told of the coming plan. He was, however, persuaded to join in with the others as they began to gamely prepare their feast.

Several had to start over as their attempts to cut the icky crust off their bread went terribly awry. Finally, all of the misshapen snacks made it into the oven for a little baking magic. When the sandwiches were finally removed from the baking apparatus, the picky eater mentioned before, eyed his snack suspiciously as the rest of the students dug right in. Peer pressure persuaded him to take a miniscule bite followed by another and another. He then cheerfully declared himself a "real good cook." Score one for that!

Cool Conversations

During a celebration of the 100th day of school, one of the activities was to cut items out of magazines that the children would purchase if they had $ 100 to spend. Sometimes the best intentions backfire marvelously! All went well until the class got the “snickers” when one of the kids found an overlooked underwear ad.

Suddenly an eight year old was shouting cheerfully, as the ad was waved over his head, “Look, I’m gonna’ put a bra on my page!”

Tis the stuff of memories!

* * * * * * * * * *

The neat thing about teaching at a small school is that in many cases siblings see each other quite a bit and can even sit near each other on many occasions.

On one day, a sixth grader showed his disdain toward his younger brother when he commented like this, “Did ya’ hafta spit directly on my hand? You were just like ‘psstt’ and now there is actual spit dripping on my hand! EWWWW!”

Thankfully, the Red Cross did not have to be called in for this obvious spittle emergency.

* * * * * * * * * *

Trying to explain the intricacies of government is always a challenge. And then, if one is trying to inform a very precocious fourth grader about who pays taxes in our country, then everything gets more complicated. The child was outraged as were the rest of his fellow classmates when he discovered that not everyone paid taxes. Church groups and nonprofit companies are of course exempt.

"What about the Cat-holl-ics like the priests and "nums?" the child asked. "Do "nums" pay "taxis" too?"

Sometimes it is really hard not to laugh a little.

* * * * * * * * * * *

One day two of the preschool students barreled off of the church van and came racing down the hall to screech to a halt in front of two surprised teachers.

The first child looked up and said, "That boy back there has a bunch of nasty stuff in a thing."

With that the little urchin raced on down to her classroom leaving us just looking at each other.

The other child had more information as she spoke up saying, "He's got them "crawbabs" and if you reach in there, they could just pinch your fingers clean off!"

Hooray for crawdads and other creepy crawlies that make for interesting conversations!

* * * * * * * * * * *

During a lesson in agriculture, I was leading a discussion on the amazing uses of the soybean when one of the students mentioned that soy sauce was made of the famous bean. The rest of the students had never heard of soy sauce, so I mentioned it was used in Chinese food.

One student remarked, "I hate Chinese food. It smells so wicked!"

What do you think? Does Chinese food smell wicked? I'm not totally sure that he knew what he was talking about!

* * * * * * * * * *

One day, a kindergarten student raised her arms in a nice stretch causing the shirt she was wearing to creep up, showing a bit of skin.

This "indecent act" caused a first grader to fuss in outrage, "Hey, would you pull that shirt down?!! Good grief! There is nothin' left to imagine."

That leaves us with the question, just what does a first grader think that a kindergartener has up there anyway?

* * * * * * * * * *

Once, we were reading a story in which the male character in the tale removed his shirt due to the very warm weather. This appalled the first grade boys in the class.

"Oh gross!" they screamed. "That's just nasty to walk around NAKED! You should never have that shirt off unless your swimming' or something."

The teacher was put in her place quite quickly.

* * * * * * * * * *

This conversation was overheard as two preschool students practiced for the ever—important spring graduation ceremony. One child was kind of clowning around waiting for his name to be called when Child Two had had enough.

Turning, he grabbed his friend's face with both hands. Squeezing the chubby cheeks hard enough to make the poor child's lips pucker, the offended party stated quite plainly, "This is an extremely important event. Do NOT screw this up for me!"

* * * * * * * * * *

A person can learn many important lessons from children if they are only patient enough to pay attention. One lesson is the simple joy that youngsters can find in small events.

One fifth grader, in an exceptionally good mood for some reason, announced to the class on one of the many trips out of the classroom, “Come on everybody! Let’s go up the hallway like spirited pixies!”

He then proceeded to “frolic” up the hall in such a way that made him appear possessed. At least he was a “pixie” with a smile on his face!

* * * * * * * * * *

Every teacher dreams of teaching the lesson that excites and inspires the students in his or her class. However, the problem comes when the students are excited and inspired by something the teacher cannot understand.

For example one day I was using the good old pull down map of the United States to use up “those little teachable moments” that all college professors are always talking about. Using a yardstick, I located the state of Illinois and pointed it out as the state we lived in. Suddenly, a hand shot up into the air.

As I looked up, an excited voice asked, “Teacher, what’s that red line?”

I couldn’t see what the big deal was, but I explained that the line divided our fair state from Iowa, Kentucky, Indiana, etc. Suddenly the room had erupted in a buzz of enthusiastic chatter that should have given me great pleasure as an educator.

One problem though—I was completely out of the loop and had absolutely no idea what the children were so excited about.

Hands shot up all over the room and words tumbled over each other as the kids shouted phrases like, “Oh cool!”

“Can we go there?”

“We could use a plane or something!”

“Can we stand on it or touch it?”

I felt like I had just stepped onto an alien planet or something as I tried to make order out of chaos.

“Hold it.” I said rather loudly to be heard over the noise. “Go where and do what? I asked as the voices died down to an excited hum.

“To the red line!” stated the little urchin who started the excitement as heads across the room bobbed in agreement.

They wanted to go and stand on the line that divided our state from the others. The scary part was that all of them thought of the idea at the same time.

Lesson learned—there is always a chance that students will catch the teacher off guard, especially if they are looking for the “thin red line.”

* * * * * * * * * *

Children also teach us new vocabulary words. One day a kindergartener came streaking out of the bathroom. Apparently, there was an eight-legged creature in the corner, but that information was a bit hard to gain from the words that came out of his mouth.

“Teacher, come fast,” he shouted. “There’s an enchilada in the bathroom!”

The Mexican entrée is probably not what he meant though, with the varied experiences of what actually could be in the boys' bathroom in a grade school, it was not totally outside the realm of possibility.

* * * * * * * * * * *

While helping out watching the kids before classes began, one school board member got a little more than he bargained for. While a very nice man, he is one of those individuals that could often talk the ear right off of a brass monkey without really saying anything. He also wasn't exactly used to taking to children.

When the bus arrived, he told the students to make sure they found all of their paraphernalia. The students gathered up their backpacks and coats in a bewildered fashion and couldn't wait to go to their teacher for clarification.

"Teacher," one asked, "that guy up in the gym wants a 'pair of snails.' We need to get him some, but don't know where they are."

While an explanation was given, the students still spent most of the day looking for snails.

* * * * * * * * * * *

It is amazing how quickly children grow up and change. Teaching in a combined class gives the opportunity to have children in class for two or three years instead of just one and therefore get to know them much better. It is hard to believe how quickly the students, especially the girls, can change from "little mommies with baby dolls" to "preteen models" before a person can turn around.

One day on recess duty this change became abundantly clear. As the small charges milled around in the sunshine, the teacher suddenly became aware of a confab of young students clustered around the large shade tree. It was clear they were "playing house" and seemed to be having a very good time.

Suddenly one of the young boys who was with them came shooting across the concrete, making a beeline right for me.

"Here it comes," I thought, "the shattering of my peaceful scene."

I steeled myself for the inevitable tattle line, "Teacher, so and so did..."

However while the student was clearly upset, he did not look angry. Rather, he looked kind of embarrassed.

He skidded to a stop in front of me and muttered without looking up, "You need to do something about those girls. They are talking about something really bad!"

Sure that the girls were picking on another student, I pressed for more information.

He twisted uncomfortably in front of me, his little toes digging deep into the grass. "I can't tell you out loud," he said finally. "I'm gonna have to whisper it."

Concerned that there was more to this than I originally thought, I leaned forward so that his hands could cup around my ear.

"I think they're talking about bras!" he said in a loud stage whisper.

I had some trouble keeping my smile hidden as I realized this was a very big deal to him, and would need to be handled in a caring manner. I quietly explained that when girls got to be older, they often talked about things like that.

He looked at me with unbelieving eyes and stated quite bluntly, "Well girls are just weird!"

I did smile then, and told him that he might not always think so. He walked away shaking his head.

I had just confirmed his point. I was a "weird one of them" too!

Children are such changeable creatures. Before you can even blink, they have grown and changed into the adults they will become. We have such a little time to shape them into productive members of society. Let's do all that we can!

* * * * * * * * * * *

Even in a Christian school, there are problems with children using mean or even profane language. The real truth is that many students who go to Christian schools do not have Christian homes, as much as we would like to think differently. So, like in other schools across the country, my class had "the talk" in which we discussed the words we should and shouldn't say. Now let's fast forward a few weeks to a day where all "heck" is breaking loose in my classroom and the kids are deeply involved in "center time."

My aide had the morning off and I faced the controlled chaos alone. As I tried to help a struggling student, I heard a piercing yell as a blond head rose from behind the bookcase like a "phoenix from the ashes."

"Teacher, he just said, 'S-H-U-T-U-P!'"

While I have learned to listen and accomplish several other tasks at once, that day I just couldn't make the connection as to what the child was spelling.

"I'm sorry," I said. "I have no idea what you are trying to tell me."

The child sighed in frustration, but went back to his play and I went back to my other kiddo. Suddenly, a shriek that could pale a ghost sounded again.

"Teacher, he just said it again! He just said, 'S-H-U-T-U-P!'"

The voice was heavy with irritation and I knew I couldn't just let this go. Surprisingly, the room got quiet as I tried to sound out his spellings.

"I'm sorry," I said finally, "I just don't know what you are trying to say."

The blond head shook sadly as if the child could not believe his teacher was that dense. Finally, pointing an accusatory finger at the offensive urchin next to him, he shouted, "He just said 'Shut up.' And you said we weren't supposed to say that!"

While it was hard not to laugh that day, I did learn a valuable lesson. No one, no matter how much he or she prides himself or herself on being a good listener, there is always room for improvement! Also, it is impolite to say, "S-H-U-T-U-P" even if you just spell it.

* * * * * * * * * * *

One of the most rewarding aspects of teaching is probably teaching kids to read. What educator can deny the light that comes into a child's eyes when he or she is introduced to the wonderful world of literacy? Toward that end I, as a kindergarten and first grade teacher, I try to make reading a fun as well as fundamental part of my class. Well, one day as I was working with my kindergarten class on sounding out words, things didn't quite turn out the way I planned.

I had all of the students at the board diligently sounding out letters I told them to write. I gently led them to the word "mom."

I then put an excited ring in my voice and said, "Now, when you draw Mom a picture or write a letter, you can put her name on it!"

With that, one of my students nodded wisely and said, "Yeah, like when you give out "violent times" cards."

I froze as my mind whirled. "Violent times cards…violent times cards."

Then the light suddenly dawned. "Oh," I said, "you mean Valentine cards!"

The child looked at me strangely and repeated like his teacher had suddenly gone dense on him, "THAT'S WHAT I SAID! VIOLENT TIMES CARDS!"

Needless to say the lesson kind of went downhill from there, but now I know I can never take for granted what the kids hear.

* * * * * * * * * *

It is always amazing to me what innocent words can start the most memorable conversations. As I was walking out to the playground with a young kindergarten student one day, I noticed she was wearing a navy blue t-shirt emblazoned with the words "Fashion Diva."

In an effort to make conversation I remarked, "Hey, your shirt says 'fashion diva.' Does that mean you like shopping and clothes and things like that?"

To which she replied, "Oh, yes! You've got to love it, really love it or you aren't any good!"

"Where do you like to shop?" I asked.

"Lots of places," she replied. "But not in Evansville 'cause it takes too long to get there and get the party started."

(Note: Evansville, Indiana is a larger city about 45 minutes from the school vicinity.) When I made the comment that I didn't always care for shopping, she stated, "I'll tell Mom. Just let me know your sizes."

She then proceeded to look me up and down with a critical eye and state matter-of-factly, "You didn't care what you looked like today didja?"

To Miss Fashion Diva's credit, I chose to view the situation with humor instead of laying the child out flat, but she and I never discussed fashion any more!

* * * * * * * * * *

Just in case you had run out of things to laugh about, here is one more. One day a fifth grader's father came to enjoy the school's tacos with his son. This child's parent happened to be a "dead ringer" for the jolly man in a red suit who graces chimneys all over the world with his gracious presence.

Apparently he was very realistic to one young lady who whispered to me excitedly. "Teacher, who is that man?"

"That is a fifth grader's daddy." The teacher answered.

"He must be real busy!" the child replied.

"I guess. He is a funeral director."

At this point it should be mentioned that it had been a really long day and the poor instructor had no earthly idea where the youngster was going with this.

"Yeah, but that's just his day job, right? 'Cause I can't believe he's here eating tacos with us!"

"I'm sorry," said the teacher in exasperation, "what are you talking about?"

"He's Santa Claus!" she squealed in a whisper.

Which, by the way is very difficult to do. You ought to try it sometime! It didn't matter when her teacher told her that Santa was NOT currently sitting at the lunch table.

"After all," the teacher asked, "would Santa really be wearing a 'Hunters Rule' t-shirt?"

"That's his disguise!" The amazement could easily be heard in her voice.

When the child scraped her plate, she flew up to the poor, unsuspecting father and grabbed his leg in a massive hug.

Looking up into his face the child stated, "I've been REALLY good this year!"

A bewildered visitor replied, "That's good, honey."

He was just as confused as the teacher had been. Just a tip—Please let the children in your life keep those childhood experiences for as long as they can. They will grow up all too soon.

The Bible Says What?

Teaching at a Christian school provides a unique opportunity to use every day to spread God's word to youngsters who may not otherwise get the chance. However, sometimes well-meaning teachers bite off a little more than they bargain for in the conversations that come after.

One of the most memorable included the study of the Beatitudes. Much of the vocabulary was new to the children causing me to explain some of the new terms.

The one that caused the most controversy was the one that read, "The meek shall inherit the earth." I explained that meek meant that a person was calm, quiet, and slow to fight others. This concept made absolutely not sense to the outspoken young lady of the group.

She remarked, "That is well and good, Miss Niki, but those 'meek' people aren't going to take this world from me! I'm gonna fight for it! They'd better get out of my way."

She had obviously missed the point of the lesson.

* * * * * * * * * *

During one of my brighter insights in having the kids connect with their Bible lesson, I decided to have the students act out the story of Jesus raising Lazarus from the dead. The event went a little like this...

The student who was Lazarus curled up in the corner of the classroom covered by the beanbag "stone" that another student portraying Jesus was supposed to roll away when Lazarus was "called forth."

Well, it took more time than I thought to get the "crowd" of onlookers cued for their performance so "Lazarus" was getting pretty tired of being wadded up in the corner. His legs shot out from under the beanbag while his head and shoulders remained covered up.

One of the clever "disciples" stood looking on and remarked, "Praise the Lord! Lazarus moves, but he sure does stinketh!"

I just hope that when the Man Upstairs saw the performance, He knew the students' hearts were in the right place, even if they weren't exactly reverent.

* * * * * * * * * *

One day, one of the kindergarten students who had never been in any type of church environment before she stepped foot into our school got a very pointed lesson on the Ten Commandments, specifically the one that states, "You shall not take the Lord's name in vain."

When the puffball from her paper plate sunshine blew across the table and landed in another kindergarten crafter's lap, she said quite loudly, "Oh my God! Did you see that?"

To that, another kindergartener looked at her and spoke very seriously as he said, "Little girl," (He didn't know her name yet.), "taking the Lord's name in vain like that will send you to Hell faster than anything else."

She was duly chastised!

* * * * * * * * * *

One of the most rewarding aspects of teaching at a Christian school is the deep theological discussions that can take place. The only problem is that many times, these talks come at most inconvenient times, such as the time my students decided they had to know exactly what God looked like right before lunch time.

One of my students, who always managed to ask the really tough questions, let loose with "If nobody really knows what God looks like, how will we know who He is when we get to Heaven?"

While the other students waited expectantly for my answer, I wished for just a moment that my wonderful "question asker" was born without vocal cords.

I knew the old line, "Oh my! Would you look at the time?" was not going to work.

My class was studying me like a pack of wolves considering a particularly juicy piece of meat. This inquiry deserved an answer.

I took a deep breath and faced the question head on. I explained that God is so much a part of Heaven, that there is no way we can miss Him. He is essentially Heaven itself. As the students began nodding, I thought I had fielded that one rather well as we bowed for prayer and then gathered our things for our daily trek to the lunchroom.

I breathed a sigh of relief and got ready to lead my charges when the same voice stopped us in our tracks. "So, is God black or white?"

Needless to say, we were a little late to lunch that day.

Children see the world differently than adults and all of us "big people" are sometimes caught off guard by that whole idea. Their natural curiosity is not to be dealt with by cowards. Who knows, maybe when I get to Heaven I'll end up asking God for His I.D.!

* * * * * * * * * *

During a week-long discussion on the Ark of the Covenant, which was the box that contained the Ten Commandments, I fully explained what the sacred box was for, what it contained, and the special instructions for handling it.

The fact the kids found most amazing was that if a person touched the ark and was not a priest, he or she would drop dead instantly. I thought nothing of this information until the week's culminating event. I attached a large box to two yard sticks with masking tape and assigned the roles of Moses, priests, and Israelites to the class. We then paraded through the school telling each class a fact we learned.

As we were crossing the gym floor, one of the lowly "Israelites" reached out a tentative hand to touch the "Ark." Of course, nothing *really* happened, but obviously the rules had made an impression on one of the "priests."

He shouted, "Well, way to go! You just dropped dead!"

That was one instance when the student was *much* too comfortable in the role he was playing. Bible lessons were kind of dull for a while after that one!

Lights, Camera, Action!

Picture day is one of the highlights of the school year and requires teachers to mind the parents admonitions to "keep the shirt tucked in, straighten the bows, make sure my child wears the jacket, etc." Of course the students themselves have their own stresses about what they are wearing and how they look.

One young gentleman entered the classroom on one particular picture day with a terrible frown on his face. While I was thinking about how terrific that face would look on his photograph, he gave the reason for his displeasure.

"I don't understand why every time I get my picture taken, my parents dress me like a dork."

In all fairness to Mom and Dad, the shirt and tie combo was very nice and looked exceptionally good on their son. Telling the child this did nothing for his outlook however, since most students showed up in shorts and t-shirts.

He even announced to the photographer that she would just have to do the best that she could since he was looking "Totally Dorky!"

When the pictures came back, the little urchin was secretly pleased when his picture was the one all of the girls requested. Turns out it wasn't a totally disgusting outfit anyway.

* * * * * * * * * *

School programs are also the stuff of memories where everyone, for however brief a moment, gets to become a star. Leading up to the big moment has its challenges, however, such as this one Christmas memory. The children managed to bring up all kinds of issues that we frankly hadn't thought of.

"If I am the 'head angel,' one said, "Does that mean I can push the others around?"

"If I have to play the mom and he has to play the dad, does that mean people will think we are married?"

And after singing the second verse to *O Little Town of Bethlehem*, "What are the 'mordals' and why do they sleep and not notice the angels?"

No wonder the word "program" brings added stress to educators.

* * * * * * * * * *

During a practice for the performance of "God's Perfect Plan," rehearsals were anything but ideal. The students had spent a week stationed at the church instead of the school due to major heating issues, so when the teachers finally got their little charges in the gymnasium and onto the stage to practice, their drill instructing teachers managed to practice for two hours straight with them and not even realize it.

In fact, these same teachers in their infinite lack of wisdom or sympathy, kept picking at the children to stand up and sing out before they looked down to notice that the children had been on their feet singing their little lungs out for over one hour straight! OOPS!

We also had another catastrophe during this marathon sing along. One of the second graders was standing near the tip top of the tree (right under the stage lights) and managed to overheat and pass out! The poor kid said when she came too, that she felt just like a McDonald's

French fry! There is nothing like getting to practice those first aid skills for real!

In spite of all of this, the program went off without a hitch in front of a packed house and all the teachers said, "Amen!"

"Look What I Made!"

The Open House is always a great way to let the students show off their creative talents. One such project occurred when the older kids made Native American dioramas to show parents what they learned in history class.

The students were super excited about collecting "supplies" to make their construction paper teepees more authentic. The teacher figured the class would collect dried grass or maybe small flowers for their boxes, so after giving everyone a plastic shopping bag, they headed out. The instructor, however, underestimated the creativity of her charges.

Whole tree limbs and hapless weeds ripped out by the roots quickly made their way into bags and into the building. By far the greatest find, though, was this lovely plant with the soft golden foliage at the tip. This wonder plant made dandy "trees" as the stems were stout enough to glue in the corners of the boxes. They also put out a lovely herbal scent. (That's right you botanist experts. The children, in their infinite lack of wisdom, brought perhaps thousands of goldenrod spores into the school!)

It created a virtual golden cloud in Miss Roethe's room and the class spent the next four days with itchy eyes and runny noses. What FUN! And it was all in the name of education.

* * * * * * * * * *

During one activity, the K-1 class made paper mache' Liberty Bells. With the smaller class size, it was supposed to be "no big deal." Those were the famous last words of a naïve teacher.

But let us not kid ourselves. Six children, liquid starch, and newspaper can still make one whale of a mess. I thought the boys would get into the project while the girls would be a little hesitant to get so dirty.

Well, that is just another area where my teaching experiences have led me astray.

The girls just dove in while the guys barely touched the starch before whining, "OOOH it's so sticky! My hands feel gross. Can I go wash now?"

The highlight, of course, was spray-painting the bells with gold paint. I put rubber gloves on each child and then took them out one at a time for the painting.

One boy was extremely impressed with his gold-gloved fingers. He told me that he planned on cutting those fingers out of the gloves and selling them for money.

I'm not exactly sure how that panned out. Some things one just doesn't need to know!

* * * * * * * * * *

For the annual open house one year, we traced all of the children on large butcher paper and had them create likenesses of themselves to place at their desks for the parents to see. We much preferred these paper children to the real ones!

With all of them spread out on the floor for the children to color, it looked to the untrained eye like a massive crime scene. The children did do a fairly good job creating themselves even if one of them ended up coloring his face green and several ended up with super huge eyeballs that dominated the entire head!

The parents were pleased so I guess that is what matters.

Imaginations Gone Awry

During a Valentine party, I took all of the students up to the gym and gave them a drinking straw. Contestants were to then place the straw in their mouths and carry a paper heart on the end of it by sucking air through the straw to create a vacuum effect.

The children were enthusiastic even if they were less than skillful. Most of the students were laughing too hard to actually succeed at the game. However, as time went on, I realized that three of our young men had actually made it to the far end of the gym without apparent difficulty. I was simply amazed at their lung capacity and told them so.

When I got close enough to observe the boys, however, I realized that the plastic straws had skewered their poor, pink hearts so that the creative youngsters could still breathe. While technically cheating, you had to admire the students' ingenuity.

* * * * * * * * * * *

It is amazing how an overactive imagination can trigger a major meltdown. This is a case in point.

A student in my class once believed he was shrinking. I kid you not. The child was terrified. He had spent the night with his cousin and both arrived at school early so that they could play in the gym before classes started for the day.

In their haste to get to their respective classrooms, the boys inadvertently picked up the wrong jackets, which happen to be identical. Everything was cool until recess time when the younger, and smaller of the two boys went to don his jacket. He was deeply disturbed to discover that the sleeves of the jacket totally covered his hands.

"Miss Niki," he wailed. "Call Mom quick! I'm shrinking!"

It turns out that his older and much larger cousin had the smaller coat in his locker and the disaster was averted. It did, however, call for a few tense moments and I tried very hard not to laugh.

* * * * * * * * * *

One early spring day the students were outside using sticks to dig into the plethora of molehills as they explored their world. Low and behold when one enterprising youth dug a little deeper into the soil, his stick came up covered with black, sticky mud. Of course he came to a completely logical conclusion.

"Black Gold!" he screamed as the other little entrepreneurs start dancing and singing, "We struck OIL! We struck OIL!"

Before their teacher could set them straight they had already made plans to build a drilling rig so that they could cash in on their new-found wealth. They were sorely disappointed when they discovered that oil is at least several hundred feet underground and not a couple of inches. In spite of this information the children still held onto their dreams and planned for a drilling operation for several weeks after sticking that first limb in the mud!

After all, teachers can't know everything!

* * * * * * * * * *

While studying a unit on plants, I placed different "mystery seeds" in Ziploc baggies. The assignment was to draw what kind of plant grew from the seeds. I underestimated the investigative powers of my students.

Someone discovered where I had placed the answer key and informed everyone which bag had the dill seeds in it. Of course, everyone knows that dill goes along with pickles, but none of the students ever associated "pickles" with the cucumbers that grow on the vine.

That is why, when the pictures were turned in, there were vibrant "palm tree like" plants with large "pickles" swinging in the breeze! Under the cheerful depictions on every page was the word "dill!"

At first, I was upset that someone had "discovered" the answers, but then I realized that if the children had not seen that dill was among the "mystery" seeds, I would not have seen the pickle trees created before my eyes!

I am truly grateful that sometimes God lets me see things through the eyes of students. I will never again be able to buy a jar of pickles without remembering the day when those pickles grew on trees!

* * * * * * * * * * *

One thing that I discovered when I first started teaching, was that children today, raised on computers and video games, often have no idea how to use their own imaginations to entertain themselves.

They tend to look to others and say, "So, find something to amuse me!"

Therefore, I placed "the house" in my classroom.

Originally an old wooden puppet stage that my dad collected from the junk pile at the school he taught at, the house survived our wild and wooly grade school days and became everything from a grocery store, to a bank, and everything in between.

With plenty of "play" left in it "the house" was installed in my classroom as an effort to teach my children how to use the brains God gave them.

In one of my more creative moments, I turned the playhouse into a space command center to coincide with our study of space in science. I found an old computer keyboard, some old earphones, and plenty of space posters to hang up to remind the students of "intergalactic" travel. My aide completed the center with welding gloves, binoculars, and goggles that she collected from her house. With that, our group was ready to "blast off!"

For two weeks I got rather used to hearing phrases such as,

"Let's jump into hyperspace!"

"To infinity and beyond!"

"Get him with your phaser!"

And, "Houston, we have a problem!"

While I was used to the extra noise and the unique phrases that the students used to make their space station a success, I was unprepared for the vision that awaited my eyes on one fateful day.

One of my younger students slipped the goggles over his head getting ready to leap into space.

Little did he know, however, that another student had tightened the goggle straps all the way and managed to somehow attach the welding gloves to the sides of the goggles. When the aforementioned "spaceman" slipped into the now very snug goggles, the welding gloves protruded from the sides of his head like puppy dog ears! Orson Wells would have been so proud!

There, in front of me, was my very own alien wearing a huge smile and of course, very unusual "ear gear!"

I don't know if there are aliens on other planets or not. If there are some sorts of beings from other planets, however, I hope they're all as cute as my own little spaceman. It is amazing how creative computer fed, video game suppressed, children can be if they are given half a chance.

Animal Trials

What happens when a dead mole is found on the playground? When teaching in the country, this phenomenon does occur on occasion.

I was not exactly sure how the poor creature met its demise, but the students were concerned. I don't even want to know how it "traveled" across the playground to land at my feet, but suddenly, there it was!

The locators wished to take it into the building for further study, but the more compassionate souls wished to have a funeral.

"Shouldn't we say somethin'?" one youth shyly inquired.

One youngster, the local undertaker's son, remarked, "I can take it home. We can try out some of my dad's stuff on it!"

Much to the observers' consternation, I simply obtained rubber gloves from the kitchen and tossed the small creature into the dumpster. Many mourning students were then forced to form lines and file back into the building feeling that the soul of the mole was in jeopardy.

The excitement was still high when the children encountered my sister indoors. The following statements were spoken rapidly.

"We found a mole on the playground."

"It's dead!"

"It looks weird and smells BAD!"

"Can we bring it in?"

"Can we? Can we?!"

With that glowing endorsement, the teacher firmly said, “NO!”

By the way, the children still want to know where a mole’s soul goes. Do you have any answers?

* * * * * * * * * *

Because the school has an open field behind it, the school has had over the years an almost constant stream of wildlife.

One day as the children were completing their normal, “Let’s run screaming across the playground routine” they found a new pet. They hauled me over to see their new friend that appeared to have been injured.

The feline was dragging its back legs. It had either been in an accident or had some sort of genetic problem. The compassionate little souls in our classes insisted something should be done by someone and that someone was supposed to be me.

I explained to the children that the cat was resting and we should leave it alone. Hopefully, it would find its way home.

In my head, I was praying “Please, God. Help this cat go home!”

Once I got the kids distracted by play, they appeared to forget about the poor beast. God does answer prayer as the poor feline never appeared again.

* * * * * * * * * *

On another occasion, a much healthier feline began visiting the playground at L.C.S. The animal seemed to have the uncanny ability to know just when the students stepped outside the door. (Of course, that would not be too difficult as the students scream like paroled convicts every time they are released to go outdoors.)

At any rate, this cat was extremely friendly and never scratched the students, even though he had just cause! Well, the friendship lasted for about two weeks before one of the kindergarten students decided that Kitty needed a ride on the merry-go-round.

It should be noted that the teacher at the time was at the other end of the playground and while she shouted warnings, they went totally unheeded.

Let's just say that I now know what true terror looks like as I watched in horror as that poor feline's eyes were bulging from its sockets as its claws clutched the wooden boards tightly while it was whipped around through several enthusiastic revolutions.

When the ride finally wound down, that cat staggered from the bench, totally ignoring the students' entreaties for it to stop and lit across that playground like its whole backend was on fire.

We never saw that poor animal again, but if he is still around, you can bet he remembers the L.C.S. students less than fondly!

* * * * * * * * * *

Classroom pets are a great learning experience for students. That, at least, is what the teacher, the animals' primary caregiver, tells herself or himself each day. When, however, the classroom hamster turns up missing, it leads the instructor to question whether or not the idea really has merit.

One day, I entered my room at 7:00 a.m. like normal and quickly began my preparations for the day ahead. It did not take long to realize that something was wrong. I noticed that the lid of Snoopy the Hamster's cage was askew and that his "recreation ball" that we had for him to roll around in was on the floor. I looked at the cage in shock, but I couldn't manufacture something that just wasn't there. Snoopy was missing.

Calmly telling myself not to panic, I took a deep breath and very quickly flew off of the handle. Just short of calling out the National Guard, I hollered for my sister and called my aide at home, pulling her from a well-deserved cup of coffee to join in the search.

We checked the room from top to bottom, but found no evidence of the furry rodent. I finally had decided that he must have crawled up into the heat register. We would not know if my theory was correct until the heat would kick on for the day. I was not looking forward to smelling hamster ham hocks all day, but I was more concerned with how to tell the kids that their beloved pet was gone.

As I quietly thought out my sorrowful words for the children, I noticed a bookshelf with a small gap at the bottom. Had we looked under that shelf? I got down on my hands and knees on the floor, peeking under the shelf and fully expecting the worse. There was Snoopy, his small beady eyes staring at me as his nose twitched as if to say, "Well, it took you long enough!" The bookcase was quickly moved and Snoopy was gently placed back in his cage.

By the time the children entered the room a few minutes later, Snoopy was "pigging out" on his breakfast and I was much calmer.

Although Snoopy has since gone on to his Heavenly reward, he does bring back many fond memories. Also, he has led me to rethink the idea of classroom pets.

* * * * * * * * * *

I once read that having an aquarium with fish often calms more restless individuals and I enjoy watching fish myself. I have decided that fish make good pets, and the bonus is that at any given time, they will be the quietest members of your classroom, guaranteed.

With this thought in mind, I had a friend search the yard sales to find a good used aquarium. I contributed some cheap gold fish and a parent donated a large fantail fish. With that contribution and a container of fish food, we were ready to dive right into the world of aquatic life.

The children really enjoyed feeding them and I enjoyed the fact that the kids were excited. We became a fairly close-knit group and the year was going at a pretty good clip. Then the inevitable happened.

I had noticed that the donated fantail was swimming kind of slowly for a few days and seemed to be getting fat. I assumed that it was going to lay eggs or something. After all, I am just a teacher. My marine biology education has been lacking. I left on a Friday, never dreaming what I would find on Monday when I entered my classroom.

As I came in, I gave the hamster a glance to make sure that he was in his cage like he was supposed to be and then moved on to the fish. There, I met a very gross sight. The fantail fish was completely white, its scales having fallen off sometime during the weekend. It was swelled to enormous size due to the water it had apparently absorbed, and it was still alive!

I decided that there were some things that the kids didn't need to see, so I quickly got a paper towel and the green fish net, fished out the bloated body and headed to the bathroom to send the "fishy" to a watery grave somewhere else.

I then tried to figure out how to inform my students since; being a larger and different colored fish, the fantail's absence from the tank would be immediately noticed.

As the kids entered the room, I fended off inquiries until everyone was assembled for the day and then carefully and gently explained that the larger fish had gotten sick over the weekend and I had to get rid of it. Student response was not what I expected.

The first words I heard were, "Didja flush it?"

Believing I should be truthful, I nodded slowly.

"Well, how did you know it was sick?"

I guess they assumed there was at least a possibility that I flushed a perfectly healthy fish by mistake! I tried to spare them the most gruesome details, but did tell them a little of what I had witnessed. There next response was startling at best.

As one the class murmured, "Cool!"

Then somebody added, "Wish we could've seen that!"

There went my theory that the children would be upset. The only thing that truly disturbed them was that I had flushed the fish before they had gotten a good look!

The longer I teach, the more I have come to the conclusion that I will never truly figure kids out. I mean, I can do my best, but there are always going to be some aspects of their little brains that I just won't be able to fathom. Of course, that is probably how they see me too!

* * * * * * * * * * *

Show and Tell is always an exciting area in the field of education. Teachers everywhere stand patiently every day to watch small charges line up with their treasures to show. Of course, every imaginable thing can be a proper show and tell item, but for me, none will be as memorable as the "day of the minks."

One of my students came streaming down the hallway with some moth eaten piece of fur wrapped snuggly around his neck as he shouted, "Teacher, these here are my minks!"

And sure enough they were—real live but no longer living actual minks complete with brown little snouts, leering glass eyes and menacing fangs. As the stuffed animals seemed to track my every move, I missed the student fishing around in his pocket.

"Teacher," he asked as I pulled my eyes away from the staring minks on each shoulder to focus on the child, "could you sew this on with some of that thread in your desk drawer?"

The "this" was a missing mink foot complete with all of the little digits as well as claws.

As pleased as I was with the idea of adding taxidermy to my list of resume accomplishments, I had to refuse due to time constraints. (Yeah, right! That's just a nicer way of saying, "I love you kid, but I wouldn't touch that thing for any amount of money!")

Anyway, the little foot was a huge attraction for my class, who held it, patted it, and crooned to it like a kitten or a puppy, totally grossing me out, as the minks proper still followed my progress around the classroom from their perch atop the proud owner's shoulders.

I was finally able to get the thing out of my classroom so that I could do my job. I had mostly forgotten about the intruders and unfortunately forgot to tell the other author of these tales.

The whole school knew what she thought of the minks when the proud student brushed the loose mink foot against her hand when she was reaching to tie a child's shoe. At least the day wasn't dull!

Let's Party!

Fun doesn't start in a classroom until a teacher has held a class party. Something about the anticipation of treat bags, games and snacks do weird things to the chemical balance in the brains of children. In short, they come unhinged.

During a valentine party one year, the extremely health conscious room mother handed out bananas in the treat bags. This led to the inevitable look of shock as the children discovered they were totally without the little conversation hearts, assorted chocolates, gums, or suckers.

Still a few stern looks from their teacher kept the children reasonably still until the same mother began passing around her very special heart shaped low fat, no sugar rice krispie treat. Enter the wonderfully picky eater, who had already been burned by the no candy treat bag. Stern looks from the teacher could not stop the outburst. His whine could be heard over the din of the others exclaiming loudly over the presence of a cool yellow fruit in their sacks. (After they got over the initial shock, most were pleased.) Anyway, back to picky.

"Hey Somebody's Mom! Hey! I don't like these things!"

The krispie was waved like a flag of surrender over his head. The aforementioned teacher quickly intercepted the little hand before it could hurl the offensive snack across the room and made him understand very quickly that not accepting the treat would be rude.

The child was reminded, "Jesus sees you right now."

Thankfully, he saw the error of his ways before he ended up scraping his snack off of the wall during recess.

* * * * * * * * * *

In the spirit of giving one year, my sister and I decided to go a whole new direction during the annual Christmas party. Instead of the normal "boys buy a boy gift" and "girls buy a girl gift" we decided to have our children draw names for the annual gift exchange. Imagine the cries of dismay when some of the guys drew girl names!

"Eeww! I ain't never bought for one of them before!"

It is amazing how much children can make gender sound just like a dreaded disease. Their totally unsympathetic teachers explained that they needed to get used to it because someday, they might want to buy a gift for a member of the opposite sex. To the youngsters, this was an entirely foreign concept; however it worked out very well and has since become a holiday tradition.

Parental Problems

One of the most challenging aspects in the field of education is dealing not with the students, but their parents. It is always rather like walking a very narrow tightrope to educate the children and manage to keep Mom and Dad, or in many cases, Grandma and Grandpa satisfied with the students' knowledge and academic achievements.

There is one holiday celebration that has, over the years caused many parent complaints and concerns: Halloween. For a long time this time of year caused no problems because at a Christian school, we did not celebrate the holiday, but then there was the year of the pumpkin. I am not sure what happened; maybe it was the group of kids that we had but as soon as that October rolled around some of the kids started talking about trick or treating, costume choices, pumpkin carving, etc.

While the school does not actively celebrate the holiday, we have no problems with those who do. Children are free to talk about it if they wish, and until the year of the pumpkin, it had never been a problem. Some celebrated, some didn't, end of story, right? Wrong! That year several of the students started telling the celebrators that they would go to the hot place with the devil if they enjoyed any aspect of Halloween.

One little gem even went so far as to tell others that pumpkins in and of themselves were evil and furthermore, those with even a pumpkin on their porches, carved or not would earn themselves a one way ticket to H-E-double hockey sticks.

When asked for parental support to deal with the matter, the parents of the offended student backed their daughter's claim. When my sister did an agriculture lesson on the pumpkin, cutting it open to see the seeds, said youngster went ballistic, and even told her instructor that she would be going to Hell for opening the orange gourd.

The teacher informed her troubled student that since God made the pumpkin, it wasn't evil. However, it never made a dent.

We even had parents fuss over pumpkin pictures in the hallway that the students had colored. A few had facial features and we were asked to take them down. I had to comply as we could not offend our students' beliefs or those of their parents, but it was also extremely difficult to comfort the students who were then terrified they would be spending much quality time with the devil for dressing like angels or Buzz Lightyear to pick up candy.

Fortunately, none of the parents of students who did celebrate Halloween called to say we were infringing on their child's beliefs.

* * * * * * * * * *

One day in the lunch room one student opened a carton of chocolate milk, stuck in a straw and began sucking vigorously while tipping the carton in an ever-increasing steeper angle.

Miss "Einstein" ended up dumping milk all down the front of her new white blouse that her mother gave us strict instructions not to let her "muss."

As we frantically tried to sop up a gallon worth of milk that had flowed from the half pint carton, she looks down at her very sloppy self and said, "Oh, LOOK! The milk made a heart shape on my shirt!"

Yeah, like THAT is going to make it all better with Mom.

Hey, we're sorry your daughter stained her shirt, but look on the bright side. She was artistic enough to spill it in the shape of love just for you!

* * * * * * * * * *

Motherhood is a sacred institution and those who enter it are some of the most dedicated individuals on earth. These chosen few should be treated with a great deal of respect and compassion. However, as a teacher, I usually have more waking moments with the offspring than the mothers themselves. This can make for a very stressful existence.

For example, recently a mother called me asking how many books her "wonder child" should have arrived home with for the summer.

During the conversation the only thing that kept running though my head was, "Why should I care? It's SUMMERTIME!"

I refrained from speaking these thoughts, however, and patiently calculated the number of books the student should have.

Another maternal figure waltzed into the school office on the last day of school wondering why her child received no "superlatives" at the closing program the previous night.

Thought—"Your child is so smart he hasn't had to work for anything. I didn't want him to win everything and make everyone else upset!"

Said—"I'm sure that I overlooked giving some awards. Thanks for bringing that to my attention!"

This is not to say that mothers should not be admired. They, along with fathers have the most important jobs that anyone could imagine. That being said, mothers are a very difficult group of individuals to please. They only want the best for their children and should be loved for it even if the teacher doesn't always live up to their "ideal instructor" image. Sometimes I don't even think Jesus could hit the mark, but I continue to do the best I can.

God Always Said There'd Be Days Like This

It seems inconceivable to students that teachers are in fact human. Instructors do in fact have feelings and can experience the same types of frustrations as their young students. And some days, it just seems as if the world would be a better place if we had just stayed in bed. These are some of those times.

After pounding the idea of adding into the brains of my kindergarten class for several months, I then began to introduce the concept of "subtraction." The class was totally against the idea of "take away" as they had been "plussing" numbers for a long time.

The radical change in instruction caused many creative ideas of dealing with the issue among the children.

One day, a youngster announced happily, "Hey guys! I got this take away thing down. Look at my easy way!"

Of course all of his classmates eagerly embraced his new way of doing the bad problems. The young man had carefully changed all of the minus signs into addition ones! How's that for quick thinking?

Of course the problems were *wrong*, but you have to admire his ingenuity. It only took the teacher two weeks to retrain the students in what it took him five minutes to teach.

* * * * * * * * * *

Sometimes it really doesn't matter what you say as an educator. There just are no words. One week, the sixth grade group was studying words from other countries in their spelling lessons.

Without giving it thought, I carefully pronounced the word "European" for my students just to find that they all collapsed into giggles.

It was then that I realized that the slang of Southern Illinois had reared its ugly head as the children heard, "You're a peein'!"

It was the big joke around the bathrooms all week long, but on the upside, even the third grade students in my class learned how to spell this new and sophisticated vocabulary word!

* * * * * * * * * *

One day one of the students managed to throw his orthodontic device into the trash during lunch. Now, in all fairness to this child, he was only six and dental devices are a big responsibility, but he could have noticed it was missing *before* the trash was taken out after lunch.

In fact, the missing equipment was not noticed until almost an hour after the trash hit the dumpster.

All of a sudden the child places his hands in his mouth and shouts, "Someone stole my retainer!"

Yep, you guessed it kiddo. Everyone is standing in line to take your retainer out of your mouth! Yuck!

Anyway, it didn't take long to discover where it had to be, so young Einstein had to go out to the dumpster, with supervision, of course, and go through all the garbage!

By then it was raining as well. Lessons were learned, however. He never threw his retainer away again.

* * * * * * * * * *

Teaching students responsibility comes in many forms. One of these occurred at L.C.S. while the elementary students were charged with the task of setting up tables and chairs for the annual chili supper fundraiser.

The teachers thought it would be a good idea for the students to help with something that would directly benefit the school and ultimately the children themselves. While I am positive that the students learned much about teamwork and perseverance in accomplishing tasks, I feel that the teachers, by far, learned the most as it took an almost Herculean amount of patience to keep everyone headed in the same direction without killing anyone.

For instance, they learned that if eight kindergarteners decide to drag a standard size folding table up the hallway, more progress is made if they all pull in the SAME direction. I realize that this is an elementary concept for most, but for some, this causes a real brain cramp.

Many of the other elementary students discovered while putting crackers on the table, that the saltine itself is rather delicate. They learned this, of course, after crushing several tubes in over zealous grips! And the teachers managed to get their respective work crews to finish the job without loosing their cool completely. And therein lies the miracle!

* * * * * * * * * *

Imagine this. Arriving at school early one morning, instead of hearing the great coal beast of a furnace doing its normal rumbling as it warms up for the day, you hear the bag and clang of hammers on metal.

One day, apparently the furnace had become ill during the weekend leaving the school a toasty 38 degrees. A school board member greeted us with the cheery news, “Y’all will be going up to the church for classes today.”

Now those of you with kids, or who are currently, or have ever been in the field of education know that relocating youngsters and placing them in an unfamiliar environment will only cause havoc. However, as staying at the school was not an option; the church was our only solution.

We gamely had all of the kids load up the paperwork that they would need for the day, packed our teaching satchels with 100 pounds of supplies a piece and walked the three blocks to the church.

There, both elementary classes proceeded to hold classes in a fellowship hall consisting of four folding tables and a wooden "slidey" curtain. As the square footage of the whole room was only slightly larger than a two car garage, getting to know each other was putting it mildly.

It was just going to be a day, and then maybe two, but our fun church experience lasted a solid week. The children did fairly well under the circumstances, but the teachers' nerves got noticeably frayed. The church meant no gymnasium, and no playground to get the wiggles out except for the parking lot.

We did get to implement some creative teaching as we taught the children how to "snake" through the church pews in the sanctuary. We figured that due to the extenuating circumstances, God forgave the extra noise. No one even swam in the baptistery, so everything turned out okay. It did make us extremely grateful for the drafty old school house and cantankerous furnace when we were finally permitted back in.

* * * * * * * * * * *

Once a student finally clobbered on my sister's last daily nerve. With her patience gone with the student who absolutely refused to keep his hands off the other students in class, the stressed teacher jerked a chair from the table, pulled the offensive being across the room, plunked him unceremoniously into the seat, and gave him the command, "Sit."

Of course, like with the training of any young individual or animal, she didn't automatically expect him to stay. She just merely thanked God that for the moment, he was not hanging from the neck of another child. Willing her voice to stay calm, she informed him that he would sit there and think. Then she took the rest of the students outside for the final recess of the day.

Apparently, the command "think" led this student through very uncharted waters as he was still parked in that chair forty minutes later when he had to be fetched by another instructor in time to catch the bus. The student suffered no ill effects from his time in solitary either. His brain apparently was able to handle the unaccustomed exercise.

* * * * * * * * * *

And then there was the fourth grade student that was trying to fix a hole in the jeans she had purchased from a recent yard sale. After obtaining the needed materials from her "always prepared" instructor, she began stitching vigorously. The enterprising student, forgot, however, about a very important piece of advice that her teacher had given her concerning the location of the hole and promptly sewed her new blue jeans to her underpants.

Of course, the student then inevitably had to go to the bathroom, prompting her teacher and a couple of well meaning girl friends to follow her to the girls' restroom to cut her free.

Luckily, there were a couple of nice sized safety pins in the office first aid kit that could be used to hold together the hole in her jeans as well as the newly made hole in her underwear.

The adventure never ends.

* * * * * * * * * *

For some reason spring seems to fly by in schools and for some students, their brains seem to fly away as well. Consider this example.

While giving a math test to some kindergarten and first grade charges, a harassed instructor looked over to see a little blond fly away kiddo on her knees in her little kindergarten chair with her nose poking between her legs. As no one else had noticed yet, the teacher hustled across the room to ask just what she thought she was doing.

To the inquiry, she replied in her little sprite like voice, "I was just a smellin' my seat."

No the instructor did NOT ask what her seat spelled like. She simply asked if she was satisfied and could go back to her test.

"Yeah," she replied, "it smells okay."

With that her little feet plopped back down on the floor and she began to work on her math facts.

If anyone out there wants to try this stunt and let these authors know what a seat actually smells like—well we'll be waiting with breathless anticipation.

* * * * * * * * * *

One Monday morning right after school started one year, someone considerately smooshed a huge granddaddy of a skunk right in front of our school. With the exhaust fan pulling in the outside air, the whole building was perfumed.

The kids noticed it right away, but of course there is always one who is more vocal.

Coming out of his classroom, he immediately clutched at his nose saying, "OOOH man! What is that incredibly bad stench? Did someone mess their pants or what? I wish I could claw my nose off!"

Of course, dramatics aside, it did smell bad enough at school that day to curl a few eyebrows. (However, we did not even notice the hot kid odor, so score one for that!)

* * * * * * * * * *

Any teacher can probably tell you about a time when a well planned lesson doesn't exactly receive the desired results. Although this has happened to me several times during my career, one incident stands out clearly in my mind. It's like a nightmare that never really goes away!

I have always enjoyed doing art projects with the kids with the exception of one time. We were creating contrast pictures with light and dark colors of construction paper. I had made my own example and carefully explained the procedure on the chalkboard using various different colors of chalk. From there, we just plunged right in!

Almost at once, my ears were tormented with cries of woe.

"I can't do this!"

"This is harrrd."

"Mine's trash! I'm throwin' it away!"

But this wasn't the worst part. As I was trying desperately to bail out the quickly sinking ship, the tears began to flow. Several of my struggling artists had collapsed under the pressure of failure.

The question I was asked most often was, "Why did you do this to us?"

To which I testily replied, "*Because I thought you would enjoy it!*"

Eventually, the class did enjoy art again, though to this day, some of my former students remind me about the "art project from Hell" which makes it live on in infamy.

But I learned a lesson that I use to this day. Anything you refer to as "easy", your students will refer to as "impossible."

* * * * * * * * * *

Sometimes it is the simplest of ideas that cause the greatest stir in the classroom. Of course, because they are simple ideas, you often neglect the most basic instructions.

Once I had a uncomplicated color mixing activity in my science center consisting of the primary colors of water in small egg cartons with eye droppers. The object was to mix primary colors together and see what other colors resulted.

I cautioned the children about squirting the colored water on the table or the floor and told them to keep the food coloring off of their clothes. I did, however, neglect one simple command.

As some of my more rambunctious students settled in at the center, they started working busily.

Then, as I watched from across the room, I heard one say, "Look, I've mixed up some poison! Let's try it!"

Then to my horror, all three little urchins tipped their heads back and squirted the eyedroppers into their mouths.

Immediately, as one, they fell on the floor making highly realistic gagging sounds and clutching their throats with morbid enthusiasm in the pretend throws of agony.

The first thought that came to mind was that the kids watched way too much T.V. As I moved across the room to intervene, however, the whole thing struck me as funny and I had a hard time disciplining them without laughing. I had to give them credit. They got an "A" for creativity and beyond a doubt, they taught me a valuable lesson.

Don't forget to state the obvious and be aware of those lethal eyedroppers full of colored water!

* * * * * * * * * * *

Teaching in small private school; housed in a building that was a public school well before it became private over twenty years ago, means that parts of the building are forever breaking down and wearing out. However, it is some of these malfunctions that make the biggest memories for students and teachers alike.

One of these days occurred when the doorknob to the door to my classroom decided to "die" right before lunch one day. The door was closed as the chosen student for the day said our lunch time prayer. We all then lined up in anticipation of the culinary delight awaiting us up the hallway. As usual, I was heading up the end of the line trying to get my little ducks in a row. When the line was quiet, I motioned for the lead student to head out. He turned the knob and pushed. Nothing happened.

Assuming that he was just trying to get a stir out of his classmates, I nudged him out of the way in exasperation and turned the knob myself.

Nothing.

I tried again and put my shoulder into it.

Nada.

With that, some of my students began to look at each other with fear. Some produced tears believing they would starve and one began holding himself and screaming, "I gotta potty before I wet myself!"

After that, in a move that would be the envy of Chuck Norris, my "spritely" 60+ year old aide hauled off and karate kicked the door at knob level to no avail.

I quickly dialed the phone to tell others in the lunch room about our plight. I did not appreciate the giggles.

As other staff members worked to take the door off the hinges, my aide and I turned to the large energy inefficient windows. With a pair of scissors, we were able to reverse the hinges in the window frame and lift the whole glass, frame and all up high enough to allow the students to climb out the window through a 1 ½' by 3' opening to a teacher waiting on the outside. Of course, the one with the bathroom emergency got to go first.

I eyed the opening doubtfully as the staff out in the hallway assured me it was the only way. I did manage to ease my 6' body through the opening but it definitely wasn't pretty. I was really glad I wore slacks that day, as a skirt would have given my students a totally different view of their instructor.

The door was soon fixed. Order was restored. The kids, however, talked about that day the rest of the year. It even made the end of the year memory book. And I smile every time I look at that window.

* * * * * * * * * *

In an ideal world, every teacher would get a "good" class. What I mean is that the ratio of boys to girls would be pretty much the same and most, if not all, of the students would try their best even if their skill level did not allow straight A's. Let me point out, this is NOT a perfect world.

One year my class consisted of nine girls and three boys, which would not have been a problem if the boys liked each other and the girls, were not seven and eight year olds going on thirty!

By November, we all had come to the conclusion that getting along was far better than fighting all the time even if, according to the students, there were WAY too many girls and the boys could never be best buds! The girls had even begun to bond together and started sharing hair and makeup tips.

It was the latter that caused problems. After a particularly detailed discussion on a new hairstyle that one girl wanted to try, another, a future beautician, decided to help out.

All of the beautification plans conveniently collided with the daily bathroom break. When coming down the hallway with the boys, I noticed some unusually loud female voices in the vicinity of the girl's bathroom.

Upon entering, I discovered one "customer" with her head tipped back over the sink while the "stylist" prepared to work her magic.

Needless to say, the desired "makeover" never did occur.

I was wondering as I marched my charges back to the classroom, "What did they think would happen when they came back to the classroom with wet hair?"

After the day when the bathroom turned into a beauty salon, the girls no longer got to take breaks in "packs." Lesson learned: Sometimes the ideas of children can look very strange to adults, but you never know what prompted the thought in the first place.

* * * * * * * * * * *

Valentine's Day and the surrounding celebration is always a series of trade offs with teachers trying desperately inspire a friendly classroom environment while at the same time trying to stem the little voices as they "sing song" "_________and ________ sitting in a tree."

One of the ways around this problem is to have the children make valentines and mail them to their parents.

L.C.S. students are fortunate enough to have a post office right across the street from the school, so mailing valentines to parents has never been that much of a problem except of course for the hours worth of class time spent into making the creations, the laborious task of printing the addresses on the envelopes and the time consuming job of getting that pesky stamp into the proper corner and affixed firmly.

One year, after we had successfully navigated those hurdles, my charges and I headed across the street and up the sidewalk to mail our "love notes." While I stood inside the tiny post office building lifting up the students to the appropriate slot, I encountered the following adventure.

Two of my boys were getting ready to push their letters through the correct slot, when one looked at the other in near panic and said, "Where's the letter gonna' go? I think I need it back!"

With that, the speaker pushed a pudgy hand into the mail slot and tried to retrieve the lost document. While I was trying to wriggle the little hand free of the opening supposedly reserved for letters, I was praying that the "jaws of life" would not have to be called.

The postmaster tried to explain to the distraught youngster that she would make sure his letter got delivered to his parents' house.

As the small hand finally popped free from the confines of the mail slot, I assured the young postal patron that by the next day, his valentine would be waiting at his house when he got home from school.

He still did not look convinced, so my older, and much wiser student placed his hand on his classmate's shoulder and said, "Look, it's a government deal. When you get older like me, you'll be able to understand where the letter goes!"

Trust a child to cut right to the chase.

* * * * * * * * * *

Once when teaching the letters of the alphabet to a less than inspired group of kindergarteners, I noticed that some of the students were really struggling to distinguish between the lowercase "m" and the lowercase "n". While I was trying desperately to find a way to help them see the difference, my most outspoken student at the time came up with an ironclad way to tell the two apart.

"That there little "m," he said excitedly, "looks just like butt cheeks, don't it?'

There were no words I could say to that one. Strangely enough, it did seem to help the rest of them!

* * * * * * * * * *

During a study on plants, my students each planted their own sunflower seeds in individual disposable drinking cups. After the planting, I cautioned the children to go up to the bathroom and give a little water to their precious seeds. One youngster left enthusiastically but never came back.

After waiting for about ten minutes for his return, I headed up the hallway to investigate. There I found the young child holding a cup brimming with water and potting soil gamely trying to poke the now floating sunflower seeds down into the more than saturated dirt. As I exclaimed in dismay over the mess he was making he looked up.

"I tried to do it your way, Teacher," he explained, "but my seeds were just too "firsty."

* * * * * * * * * *

It never ceases to amaze me when I realize that many times older children are not more mature than the younger ones, just merely taller. One day, a fifth grade student was being especially obnoxious. He was laughing hysterically over nothing. While I was thrilled that he had found a zest for life, his constant chuckles were really disrupting the class science lesson.

In desperation I finally told him to straighten up or he would have to sit in the hallway until he calmed down all the while knowing that this punishment for this child would be a "fate worse than death."

Believing that he had no other choice and could calm down no other way, the student quickly reached into his desk grabbing some scotch tape from Heaven only knows where and taped his mouth shut.

Of course, this action had the opposite effect than what he had hoped for as he still continued to laugh, only now since his mouth was taped, he began to let out grunts and snorts not unlike a hog at a trough.

At that point, I almost believed the hog would have been quieter!

* * * * * * * * * *

During a craft activity at Bible lesson time, one kindergarten student inadvertently unscrewed the base of his school glue cap instead of the bright orange tip. He then proceeded to invert the bottle and give it a healthy squeeze. Of course the glue shot all over the outside of the bottle as well as the student's hands, desk and paper project.

While I was scrambling to gather the materials to clean up my erring student as the rest of the class looked on in dismay, the student decided to take matters into his own hands, or rather tongue.

He calmly studied the glue as it rolled down his small palm and then in an action that would have impressed kitty cats everywhere, he stuck out his bright pink tongue and carefully licked the offensive hand from palm to finger tip in one wet stroke!

While the rest of the class was noticeably "grossed out" by this display, the young urchin pronounced it "tasty," and luckily suffered no ill effects.

* * * * * * * * * *

One rainy day two of the preschool students trooped off the bus, slammed their way inside the schoolhouse and stomped into the gym where I was watching them for the morning. As they flung off backpacks and bright colored rain slickers, they turned to the astonished teacher with ugly scowls on their faces.

"I don't like him no more and can't play with him," one muttered accusingly.

When asked why, he replied in a tone that left no room for argument.

"Cause he is wearin' the wrong color shirt," he said.

Wouldn't it be nice if our problems as adults were as critical?

* * * * * * * * * *

And finally, there was the bright autumn day I was headed up the hallway when I heard the following conversations coming from the boys' bathroom.

"Ready, set, go!"

"Oh you almost got him!"

"Go, Go, Go!"

"Aw man! You missed him again!"

"Let's do it one more time."

I couldn't stop myself. I just had to know, though I had already suspected what was going on. Sure enough, when I rounded the corner into the bathroom, I found three youngsters using a poor, defenseless cricket that had come into our building to warm up for target practice! Clearly the little insect wished that he were somewhere else and the boys saw the error of their ways when they had to clean up all of their "hits and misses." One thing is for certain. Teachers are never safe from being surprised.

Little Sparrows

This is the day that You have made, and chalk dust lingers in the air.
It's just You and me together, Lord to show how much we care.
The halls are quiet now, the little footsteps stilled,
but soon they'll be coming. Am I ready to do your will?
For I know I have but a short time to put Your love upon their hearts.
I wonder if it will be enough? Will I have done my part?
Their little lives are so mixed up and that child never laughs.
That one calls me "mommy" 'cause I'm the closest thing he has.
This one needs lots of hugs, Lord. That one needs more time.
His shoes are untied again and dragging from behind.
They are all so very needy, Lord. Have I done all I can do?
Alone I cannot fix them, so I must give them up to You.
For they are all but little sparrows, resting in Your hands
and they don't have a hurt too small, that You don't understand.
Once they were strangers, the souls You entrusted to my care.
Now I have the chance, Your wondrous love to share.
Help me to do my best, Lord, and give all I can to try,
to love these kids with all my heart and teach these sparrows how to fly.

Appreciate a Teacher

Throughout the history of society, teachers have been upheld as one of the pillars of society. It is onto our shoulders that much of the weight of the future is placed whether we accept it or not. Recently however, much of our society has relegated educators to a much lower position, even though the job of these dedicated individuals is perhaps, even more important than it was just a few years ago.

It is the opinion of some, that people only become teachers because they lack the ambition to become anything else. Because of this, colleges are working much harder to assure that the teachers trained at these institutions become even more knowledgeable and are more the professionals that they strive to be. However, there are some things that as great as the programs are, no college course can ever teach. While one can be well versed in lesson plans, classroom management, and bulletin board patterns, there are some things one just can't get until he or she is in the "trenches" of his or her own classroom.

For example, what college course can prepare a teacher whose student is so excited about the coming of his baby sister and even brings pictures to show the class, when the baby that was supposed to be a Christmas joy, comes a month early, stillborn, on Thanksgiving? What words can the teacher use when she holds the student close as sobs out on another day that they just put the headstone on his baby sister's grave? There are no words for that.

What can be done for the child who confides in her teacher that her baby cousin has been abducted by her aunt's drugged out boyfriend? When the teacher tries to comfort the girl and says that God will help the police catch him, the girl looks with gentle, but unbelieving eyes and says, "Maybe, but I don't think God cares about us anymore." What college class gives words to inspire hope where there is none?

There are days when a teacher must call a parent and wake her up, so that the children will get to school that day.

Another day the teacher is faced with the questions posed by an angry student who watches his Grandpa shoot his old dog to keep it from suffering when the child knows that God could have healed his pet.

At other times an educator's well meaning Mother's Day project becomes unraveled as a student bursts out, "I don't have a mommy anymore!" and the teacher remembers too late that the child was home alone with his mom when police came and carted her away for using her four year old son to help her make her drugs.

This is a grim reminder of how we do not live in a perfect world, and many kids fall outside the boundaries of the sterile college education.

In case you are now depressed after reading this, please be assured that while all of these are true stories, most days that my sister and I have taught, have been better than these. However, it is a reminder that teaching is not for the faint of heart. The problems the children in your class face, soon become your own, and you find you will spend much of your time trying to protect your young charges from pain, while at the same time educating them of the world.

In the short time that the children are in your care, you become friend, nurse, parent, and guardian. The responsibility can be daunting, but it is very rewarding. What other profession can you mention that touches the future in such a profound way? Educators hold the power to shape young minds into the productive members of society that we wish for them to be. Every day that you teach, laugh with, and love the students, you make a difference. That is a reason to keep going even on the bad days. May God bless teachers everywhere, because when He made them, He made some very special people!